TED KENNEDY

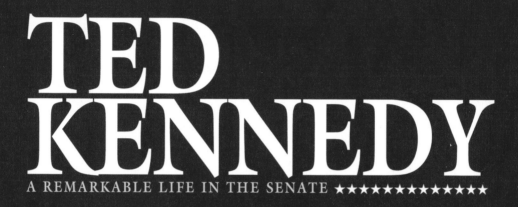

TED KENNEDY

A REMARKABLE LIFE IN THE SENATE ★★★★★★★★★★★★★★

Lisa Tucker McElroy

 LERNER PUBLICATIONS COMPANY • MINNEAPOLIS

For my daughters, Zoe and Abby, in the hopes that they will grow up to serve their country, their families, and themselves in many wonderful ways

The images in this book are used with the permission of: © Paul J. Richards/AFP/Getty Images, p. 2; © Hulton Archive/Getty Images, p. 6; AP Photo, pp. 8, 13, 17, 21, 23, 24; © Dean Conger/National Geographic/Getty Images, p. 9; © H. F. Davis/Topical Press Agency/Hulton Archive/Getty Images, p. 11; © Margaret Bourke-White/Time & Life Pictures/Getty Images, p. 12; © Alfred Eisenstaedt/Time & Life Pictures/Getty Images, p. 14; © Tim Boxer/Hulton Archive/Getty Images, p. 18; © John Dominis/Time & Life Pictures/Getty Images, p. 19; © Ralph Crane/Time & Life Pictures/Getty Images, p. 20; © AFP/Getty Images, p. 25; © Leonard McCombe/Time & Life Pictures/Getty Images, p. 26; © Herb Scharfman/Time & Life Pictures/Getty Images, p. 27; © Steve Liss/Liaison/Getty Images, p. 28; AP Photo/RR, p. 30; © Diana Walker/Time & Life Pictures/Getty Images, p. 32; © Les Stone/ZUMA Press, p. 34; © Tim Sloan/AFP/Getty Images, p. 35; © Alex Wong/Getty Images, p. 36; AP Photo/Stephan Savoia, p. 39; AP Photo/Bill Sikes, p. 40.
Front Cover: AP Photo/Chitose Suzuki.

Lerner Publishing Group, Inc.
241 First Avenue North
Minneapolis, MN U.S.A. 55401

Website address: www.lernerbooks.com

Library of Congress Cataloging-in-Publication Data

McElroy, Lisa Tucker.
    Ted Kennedy, a remarkable life in the Senate / by Lisa Tucker McElroy.
      p.   cm. — (Gateway biographies)
    Includes bibliographical references and index.
    ISBN 978-0-7613-4457-5 (lib. bdg. : alk. paper)
      1. Kennedy, Edward Moore, 1932-–Juvenile literature. 2. Legislators–United States–Biography–Juvenile literature. 3. United States. Congress. Senate–Biography–Juvenile literature. I. Title. II. Title: Ted Kennedy.
    E840.8.K35M375 2009
    973.92092–dc22 [B]   2008032325

Manufactured in the United States of America
1 2 3 4 5 6 – BP – 14 13 12 11 10 09

CONTENTS ★★★★★★★★★★★★★★★

Ted Kennedy *(left)* and his brother Bobby Kennedy laugh as they feed an elephant at the zoo in London, England, in 1938. Ted loved to visit the zoo when his family lived in London.

When I visited Ted Kennedy's Senate office, his walls told me a story. A very young Kennedy in a sailor suit was posing with his parents in one photo. A childhood photo showed him feeding elephants in Great Britain. Another photo showed him playing football at Harvard. There were photos with his famous brothers, with his wife and children, and even with his dogs. Copies of important bills he'd sponsored were framed alongside the pens used to sign them into law. Standing in the front office, a visitor feels immersed in history. It's the history of a great state, a great family, and a great senator. It's Ted Kennedy's history.

Childhood

Boston-born Edward Moore Kennedy was the youngest of Joe and Rose Kennedy's nine children—four sons and five daughters. Back then large families were not unusual. What was unusual about the Kennedy family

Joseph Kennedy *(center)* is surrounded by his wife, Rose *(fourth from left in back row)*, and their nine children. Ted, the youngest, is standing to the right of Rose.

was that three of the sons would be U.S. senators. One would serve in the presidential cabinet. Three sons would run for the U.S. presidency, and one would be elected. One daughter would be appointed ambassador to Ireland. Another would found the Special Olympics. A typical family? No. But a special one? Absolutely.

Edward Kennedy was born on February 22, 1932. On that day, the nation celebrated the birthday of its first president. The newborn's parents considered naming him George Washington Kennedy. Fortunately for him, his parents decided to name him after a close friend of his father's instead. His brothers and sisters were very excited to have a new member of the family. In fact, his fourteen-year-old brother John (known as Jack) wrote to his mother from boarding school, asking if he could be the new baby's godfather.

Young Ted was soon running around with his many brothers and sisters. He liked swimming and especially enjoyed sailing with his brothers. Brothers, sisters, and cousins often gathered at the family's oceanfront summer home in Hyannis Port, Massachusetts. They played

An aerial photograph shows the Kennedy summer home in Hyannis Port, Massachusetts.

a rousing game of touch football, a sport Ted grew to love. He was known as one of the most fun-loving members of the family. He often encouraged the others to sing and play Irish songs on the piano.

Ted Kennedy remembers well the dinner conversations of his youth. His mother and father asked the children about the day's events. Everyone would chime in. The young Kennedys quickly learned that the best way to "get the floor"—as would later be important in young Ted's Senate career—was to have "read a book, to have learned something new in school, or, as [they] got older, to have traveled to new places." He credits his parents with helping him open his mind to the world in these suppertime chats.

Ted's grandfather Honey "Fitz" Fitzgerald was an important figure in his life. The mayor of Boston, he seemed to know everyone in that city. In fact, he seemed to know everyone in Massachusetts. Ted would often walk through Boston's neighborhoods with his grandfather. He learned about the people who lived there. He learned what their needs were and how the family could represent their interests.

Ted's father was also a very influential man. When Ted was six years old, his father was appointed ambassador to Great Britain. The family moved to London, England. Ted got to know the city well—especially the London Zoo. He particularly loved petting the zebras there. (One of them once bit him on the arm but fortunately didn't do any real harm.)

Ted Kennedy *(front)* walks with family members in London in 1938, including *(back, left to right)* Kathleen, Joseph, Rose, Patricia, Jean, and Bobby. The family lived in London when Joseph was the American ambassador to Great Britain.

Ted's parents, Joseph and Rose, seem happy and outgoing in this 1937 photo.

Ted's mother, Rose, was a special person as well. She had to be to handle a family of nine active children! But she still found time to be an important participant in church work and charitable causes. In 1951 Pope Pius XII would give her the title papal countess, in recognition of her exemplary motherhood and many charitable works.

At the age of seven, Ted and his family attended the coronation of Pope Pius XII at the Vatican. At the time, Ted said, "I wasn't frightened at all. He patted my hand and told me I was a smart little fellow. He gave me the first rosary beads from the table before he gave my sisters any."

The Kennedy family poses with guards at the Vatican in Rome, Italy, in 1939. Ted is standing in front of his father in the center.

Young Ted Kennedy's family gave him many opportunities to travel and meet important people, but his parents were strict. Ted did not get a large allowance. He was not allowed to miss family meals. He and his brothers and sisters were taught to be hard working. They were expected to be modest, even though their family was so prominent. And they were taught to stand up for themselves, not rely on their family's influence. Teddy was young for his grade in school. When the older bullies teased him, his brother Robert (also called Bobby) tried to toughen him up. Bobby said, "You've got to learn to fight your own battles."

Clockwise from top: The Kennedy family, including children Bobby, Joe Jr., Patricia, Eunice, Jean, mother Rose, and Ted enjoy one of their favorite pastimes—boating.

Because Ted was the youngest child, his brothers were out of the house long before he was. When Ted was twelve, his oldest brother Joe was killed. His plane exploded on a bombing mission during World War II (1939–1945). Jack was a commander of a PT boat in the South Pacific at the time. Bobby was in a naval officer training program.

Teddy thrived in junior high. He had many friends, and he developed into a good football player. He made the honor roll during some terms. He was also known as a prankster. He and his friends sometimes played jokes on the teachers, occasionally getting caught. In eighth grade, he enrolled in a Catholic school for one year because his mother wanted him to have a solid religious education. His funniest memory of the Catholic school? Losing a footrace to a priest, who ran with his long black robes flapping about his ankles.

Getting an Education

Like all the Kennedy brothers, Ted went off to boarding school when he entered ninth grade. His brother Jack had gone to Choate, a school in Connecticut. But Ted stayed closer to home and attended Milton Academy, just south of Boston, as Bobby had done.

Ted was in the glee club and on the debating team. He also enjoyed drama. But he truly loved football. He often played on the offense and was an especially good pass receiver. His teammates relied on a play that took advantage of Ted's great strength. They would throw him the ball, let him get tackled, and then watch as he continued moving, dragging the opposing players with him across the touchdown line. They called it the lumbago pass, after a painful back condition. Very likely Ted's back would hurt afterward.

Ted suffered another loss in his life while in high school. His sister Kathleen "Kick" had volunteered for the Red Cross in London during World War II and eventually settled there. When Ted was sixteen, she was killed in a plane crash in France.

Like his brothers, Ted Kennedy went to Harvard College in Boston. As in high school, he joined the football team. He did well in his freshman year games. Unfortunately, his classes did not always go quite as well for him. Still, he learned an important lesson about honesty and integrity when he had another student take a Spanish exam in his place. Both he and the other student were expelled. Harvard told Ted that he could reapply after two years off. He had to decide what to do in the meantime.

Ted decided that he would follow in the path of his older brothers and serve his country in the military. He joined the army to fight in the Korean War (1950–1953). Instead of ending up in Korea, however, Ted was posted to Paris, France. He was an honor guard at the headquarters of the North Atlantic Treaty Organization (NATO), an alliance of North American and European nations.

After his discharge in 1953, Ted returned to Harvard. He did well in his studies and in sports. He earned a varsity letter in football in his senior year.

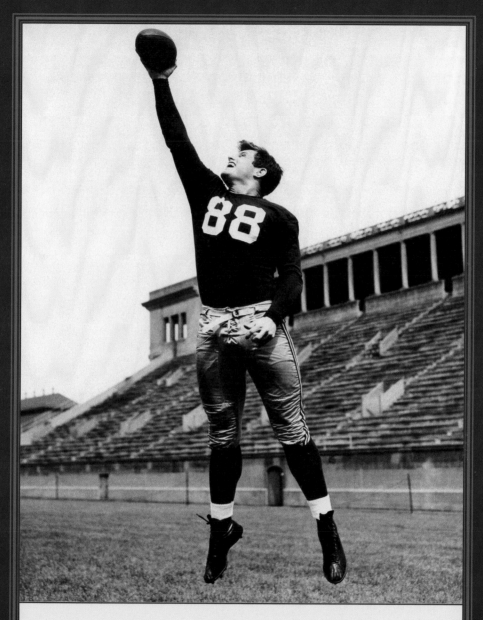

Ted Kennedy leaps for a catch during practice for the Harvard football team in 1955.

After graduation from Harvard, he attended the University of Virginia School of Law to focus on public affairs. It seemed the best preparation for the career in public service that his family encouraged.

During law school, he met two people who would be among the most important in his life: his best friend, John Tunney, and his future wife, Joan Bennett. With Tunney he would win an important prize when they placed first in the moot court, or "pretend court," competition. With Joan he would walk down the aisle.

Ted Kennedy *(left)* attends a fund-raiser in 1971 with his wife, Joan, and his best friend, John Tunney, with whom he would later serve in the Senate.

Joan and Ted Kennedy play with their two oldest children, Kara Anne and Teddy, in 1963.

Marriage and Children

Ted's fall 1957 speech at Manhattanville College in Purchase, New York, should have been pretty routine. He was just doing a favor for his older brother Jack, then a senator from Massachusetts. But he got a bonus: he met Joan Bennett. She impressed him immediately. After they dated for several months, Ted proposed during a visit to his family's Hyannis Port home. The couple was married in front of 475 guests on November 29, 1958, in Bronxville, New York.

Soon the Kennedys would welcome two children, Kara Anne and Teddy Jr. The third child, Patrick, came along a few years later. Joan enjoyed meeting new people and shaking hands. She participated actively in the political life of the Kennedys.

Working on His Brother's Presidential Campaign

When his brother Jack was running for president in 1960, Ted was right there with him. Ted traveled around the country giving speeches on his brother's behalf. He also served as campaign manager for the western states.

Primary contests were exciting for Ted. They help political parties select their presidential candidate for the general election. He worked hard to help his brother win the Democratic Party nomination. Toward that end, he attracted attention by making a 180-foot (55-meter) ski jump prior to speaking to a winter ski crowd in Wisconsin. In the summer, he actually rode a bronco to call attention to the campaign. Once, Ted spoke in place of his brother when Jack (often called JFK) got laryngitis. These activities impressed the crowds. They thought the Kennedys had guts and weren't quitters.

Kennedy speaks to a crowd at a California rally during his brother Jack's run for president.

Ted Kennedy liked to talk with local politicians to get their support for his brother's campaign. That skill made a difference at the 1960 Democratic National Convention. The states vote for their preferred candidates in alphabetical order of state name. When the tally was close to tied midway through the Ws, Ted Kennedy got a crucial assignment. Bobby, Jack's campaign manager, sent Ted to speak to the chairman of the Wyoming delegation. The assignment was to secure the last votes Jack needed for the nomination. Ted had a hard time convincing the chairman that the ballot would be that close, but he did in the end. And with Wyoming's last four delegate votes, John F. Kennedy sealed the nomination. He ran an excellent campaign. His narrow victory over Vice President Richard Nixon made Kennedy the youngest person ever elected to the presidency. He was also the first Roman Catholic president of the United States.

John F. Kennedy accepts the nomination for president at the Democratic National Convention in 1960. Ted's brother would be elected president later that year.

Having a brother elected president of the United States didn't change Ted's family. They still had a low-key attitude. Ted remembers the night before his brother's inauguration, when Washington, D.C., was covered with an unusual snowfall. He'd listened to Frank Sinatra and danced at a preinaugural ball. Then he headed home. "I remember riding back with my father and the snow had started by that time and the car got off on the side. And here was my father out pushing his car, the night before his son was going to be president, and yelling for me to push harder, to push harder."

Entering the Senate

John F. Kennedy gave up his job as senator from Massachusetts to become president at the beginning of 1961. Both John and Robert wanted Ted to fill that vacant Senate seat. But Ted was not old enough. According to the U.S. Constitution, a senator must be at least thirty years old. Ted was only twenty-eight when his brother was sworn in as president. As specified by law, the Massachusetts governor appointed someone to serve as the state's senator temporarily for a year and a half. This allowed Ted Kennedy to make plans to run for the office in 1962. Meanwhile, he worked in Boston as an assistant district attorney, or lawyer on criminal cases. He also visited Africa and Latin America to learn more about the world in preparation for his Senate bid.

Kennedy celebrates after winning his first term as a U.S. senator in 1962. His wife, Joan, is at left behind him. A picture of his brother Jack hangs on the wall behind him.

Joe Kennedy, Ted's father, was enthusiastic about his fourth son running for high public office. "You boys have what you want," he told his older sons. "Now, it's Teddy's turn." And, indeed, it was. Ted Kennedy won his first campaign for the Senate with 54 percent of the vote. In 1962 he began a career in the Senate that would span many decades.

Ted Kennedy *(center)* stands with his brothers Robert *(left)* and Jack in Washington, D.C., in 1963. At the time, Ted was a senator, Robert was U.S. attorney general, and Jack was, of course, president.

Tragedies Strike

Ted Kennedy was proud and happy to be serving in the Senate. But his happiness, at least in some aspects of his life, would be short-lived.

In November 1963, he was at the Senate when he heard the news that President John F. Kennedy had been shot in Dallas. He raced out to call Robert, who told him that their brother had died. The next several days were ones of numb shock. The surviving Kennedy sons and daughters helped their elderly parents through the ordeal while the entire nation mourned the fallen president.

Less than a year later, Ted Kennedy almost died himself. He was flying to Massachusetts from Washington, D.C., on June 19, 1964. His plane was trying to land in thick fog when things started to go wrong. Kennedy has said,

Ted (*far left*) at the funeral of his brother President John F. Kennedy in 1963. Ted stands solemnly with his brother's widow, Jacqueline Kennedy, and her children, Caroline and John Jr.

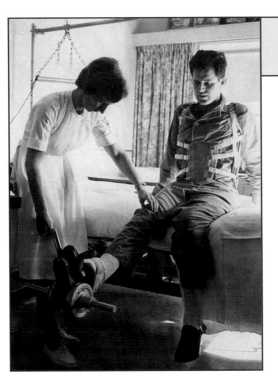

Kennedy receives physical therapy while recovering from his injuries.

"It was just like a toboggan ride, right along the tops of the trees for a few seconds. Then there was a terrific impact into a tree." But unlike a toboggan ride, this flight did not end well. The plane crashed, killing the pilot and one of the senator's aides and seriously breaking Ted Kennedy's back. Doctors believed he would never walk again. He lived in a metal frame for five months before leaving the hospital. In December he was able to return to his family and his duties in the Senate. Although the time in the hospital was difficult, Ted has said, "I never thought the time was lost. I tried to put my hours to good use. I had a lot of time to think about what was important and what was not and about what I wanted to do with my life. I think I gained something from those six months that will be valuable for the rest of my life."

But four years later, tragedy struck Ted and his family again. Robert was running for president. He had delivered a victory speech in Los Angeles, California, on

June 5, 1968, having won that state's primary. He was shot while leaving the hotel. Ted Kennedy was in a hotel in San Francisco at the time. When he saw the news on television, he raced to get a plane south to reach his brother. He got there just before doctors tried to remove bullet fragments. But despite surgery and the best medical efforts, Robert Kennedy died the following day.

After Robert Kennedy was killed, Ted Kennedy's friend Senator John Tunney of California said, "This was like a gruesome nightmare replayed and there was only darkness, I mean, just terrible feelings of emotional anxiety and depression. And I remember walking with Teddy, after Bobby died, downstairs and saying to him, 'You know, you've just got to get away.

Ted *(center in front)* helps carry the casket at his brother Robert's funeral in 1968.

Strength in Difficult Times

Although all families have hard times, Ted Kennedy and his family have had more than most. The death of two older siblings in plane crashes and two older brothers by assassination were followed much later by the plane crash and death of his nephew, John F. Kennedy Jr. He has worried as his sons, Patrick and Teddy Jr., have suffered and recovered from tumors, one cancerous. He has suffered the loss of three sisters, three brothers, his parents, his nephew, and his sister-in-law.

But what is amazing about Ted Kennedy is his spirit, even during difficult times. At his nephew's funeral, he prodded people to sing Irish songs. He encouraged his son Teddy Jr. to ski and swim after his leg amputation. He even had Teddy help him with his own skis! And he visited his sister, Rosemary, in the special assistance home where she lived for most of her life. He was at her side when she died in 2005. In the Kennedy spirit, he has sponsored legislation to help other people with disabilities.

Kennedy *(right)* with his children in 1979

You can't think about this. You can't think about it. You must not allow yourself, ever, to think about you being next in line for this terrible treatment.'" But others disagreed. They encouraged Ted Kennedy to pick up where his brothers had left off and run for the presidency. Kennedy had to weigh all the options.

It was difficult to find the right path. He often went to Hyannis Port to sail all day long so he could be alone to think. But in the end, Kennedy decided neither to drop out of public life nor to run for president—at least not yet. He said in August, "Some of you have suggested that, for safety's sake and for my family's sake, I retire from public life. To those who have so written, my deep thanks for your kindness and for your concern. But there is no safety in hiding, so today I resume my public responsibilities to the people of Massachusetts. Like my three brothers before me, I pick up a fallen standard."

A Terrible Night: Chappaquiddick

On July 18, 1969, Kennedy headed to Martha's Vineyard, an island off the coast of Massachusetts, to sail and enjoy some time with friends. Kennedy left an evening get-together with Mary Jo Kopechne. The young woman had once been a secretary in his brother Robert's Senate office. He told others he was taking her back to her motel. On the way, however, the car veered off a small bridge and crashed into a pond. The car filled with water. Kennedy escaped, but Kopechne did not. Kennedy later said that he tried, unsuccessfully, to save her.

Kennedy suffered a moderate concussion, or head injury, from the accident. It took him a while to call the police. When he did, he pled guilty to leaving the scene of an accident. He then made a public speech asking the people who elected him for forgiveness. He said, "I was overcome, I'm afraid, by a jumble of emotions, grief, fear, doubt, exhaustion, and shock." He added, "And so I ask you tonight, the people of Massachusetts, to think this through with me. In facing this decision, I seek your advice and opinion. In making it, I seek your prayers—for this is a decision that I will have finally to make on my own.... I pray that I can have the courage to make the right decision. Whatever is decided and whatever the future holds for me, I hope

Kennedy is shown on TV speaking to the public about the Chappaquiddick accident.

that I shall have been able to put this most recent tragedy behind me and make some further contribution to our state and mankind, whether it be in public or private life." The citizens of Massachusetts wanted him to continue as their senator. They reelected him to his seat in the Senate on November 3, 1970.

Then, ten years later while still serving in the Senate, he took on one of the biggest challenges of his career.

Running for President

Ever since his brother Robert's death, Ted Kennedy's name had been on the short list of presidential candidates. But not until 1980, twelve years later, did he decide to run for the top political office. He had earned the respect and support of many, but the memory of his brothers still affected him deeply.

Ted Kennedy's primary campaign started out fairly well. But U.S. President Jimmy Carter, former governor of Georgia, surprised many political commentators by gaining popularity over the course of the race. Finally, after primaries in thirty-four states, Kennedy bowed out. Still, he retained the admiration of many. "He's one of the most effective senators of this century," former Senate minority leader Tom Daschle of South Dakota has said. Representative Barney Frank of Massachusetts agrees. "If he had never had brothers, . . . he would still have had one of the great careers in American politics."

Kennedy speaks at the Democratic National Convention in 1980, announcing he was withdrawing his bid for his party's presidential nomination. Even as he ended his presidential campaign, he still smiled in thanks to his supporters.

Kennedy stepped down from the race at the 1980 Democratic National Convention, saying, "For me, a few hours ago, this campaign came to an end. For all those whose cares have been our concern, the work goes on, the cause endures, the hope still lives, and the dream shall never die."

A New Stage in Life: A Growing Family

The next decade would move quickly. He and Joan divorced in 1982. He focused his attention on his children, his brothers' children (for whom he acted as a surrogate father after the death of Jack and Robert), and his work in the Senate. But then, after many years of bachelorhood, a surprising thing happened. At least it was surprising to Ted Kennedy. He fell in love! The woman was Victoria Reggie, a thirty-seven-year-old lawyer in Washington, D.C. Their families had known each other for years—since Vicki was two years old. But they first met personally when Vicki worked as a summer mailroom intern in Kennedy's Senate office. "We met one day for three minutes, though he has no recollection of it," she has laughed. That was OK—a few years later, they met again, after Vicki had completed law school and been married and divorced. At Vicki's parents' fortieth wedding celebration, Kennedy helped her pick vegetables off the vine for a salad. Kennedy also soon came to love her two children, Curran, nine, and Caroline, six. "We were going out a lot, and Ted knew I was concerned about spending time away from my children," she said. "So one day he very politely said, 'Maybe I'll come over to your place for dinner. . . .' That started a wonderful thing. . . . I love to cook, and everyone would gather round in the kitchen, and Ted would help Caroline or Curran with their schoolwork."

★
★
★

Kennedy and his wife, Victoria, step out for a fund-raiser in July 1992, not long after they were married.

About nine months after Reggie and Kennedy started dating, he proposed at a performance of the opera *La Bohème*. "I had not ever really intended to get married again," the senator has said. "The people who had been closest to me over the course of my life had disappeared, with that enormous amount of emotion and feeling and love . . . I thought I probably wouldn't want to go through that kind of experience again." But, as he said to reporters when they announced their engagement, "I love Victoria and her children very much, and she has brought enormous happiness into my life." Vicki loved him too, and the couple married in McLean, Virginia, on July 3, 1992.

The Second-Longest-Serving Member of the Senate

In 2008 Edward M. Kennedy became the second-longest-serving member of the U.S. Senate. (Robert Byrd of West Virginia has served longer.) Kennedy's long career has been marked by hard work for traditionally liberal causes. He has been a champion of individual rights, health care, gun control, public education, and peaceful resolution for foreign policy issues.

Kennedy questions a witness during a congressional hearing at the Capitol in January 2008.

Like all U.S. senators, Kennedy has many important duties. He proposes and votes on legislation, or laws, that govern our country. He represents the interests of the people who elected him, known as his constituents. He serves on Senate committees that deal with particular areas of government policy.

A typical day in Ted Kennedy's office is extremely busy. In fact, according to his staff, he works twenty hours a day, always carrying a full briefcase as he races from meeting to meeting. Always with him, except on the Senate floor, are his two Portuguese water dogs, Sunny and Splash. He sometimes plays ball with the dogs on the Capitol Building lawn. From Tuesday to Thursday, he usually works in his Senate office. But from Friday to Monday, he is usually home in Massachusetts so that he can meet with his constituents.

Kennedy walks with one of his Portuguese water dogs outside the Capitol in Washington, D.C. Kennedy's dogs often accompany him to his office.

Most days in Washington, he attends as many as three hearings—at least one of which he'll be chairing—and several meetings. He makes dozens of phone calls and casts votes throughout the day. But he always takes the time to talk with his wife, children, grandchildren, and sisters. He is the first person to wish members of his staff happy birthday, congratulate them on an engagement, or ask about their children. He takes the time to shake hundreds of hands, take dozens of pictures, and introduce his dogs to everyone he meets.

He is the chairman of the Health, Education, Labor, and Pensions Committee. He also serves on the Judiciary Committee, where he helps select new federal judges. On the Armed Services Committee, he plays an important role in supporting our troops. Finally, he makes speeches in Massachusetts and around the country to try to make the U.S. government stronger and better.

Ted Kennedy's career in the Senate has been full of battles. He has been responsible for more than six hundred new laws. What does he fight for? Mostly he fights for those who need a strong advocate on their side. These people include those with disabilities, without health insurance, or without financial security. They include women, gays and lesbians, immigrants, people of color, and people with strong religious beliefs.

Senator Kennedy has won many of these battles. In the 1960s, he carried on his brothers' mission of ending racial discrimination. His first major Senate speech was in support of the Civil Rights Act of 1964. Since the 1970s, he has worked to help women get equal pay for equal work. In the 1990s, he was at the forefront of a law that allowed new moms and dads to stay home with their newborn or newly adopted children. In 2001 he led Congress in passing the No Child Left Behind Act. The law requires schools to test students to measure their progress. In 2007 he led the fight to raise the minimum wage for the first time in many years—and he won. And now? He's concerned with making sure that all Americans have access to good, affordable health care. He's been fighting that fight for many years in honor of his sister Rosemary and his sons, Patrick and Teddy Jr. His family members were fortunate in the quality of health care they received. Ted Kennedy wants to make sure that all Americans have access to good health care when they need it.

Looking Forward

Ted Kennedy is known as the lion of the Senate because he fights so hard for the causes he believes in. But on May 20, 2008, he received news that he would be facing the biggest fight of his life: the fight against brain cancer.

Earlier that week, Kennedy had suffered a seizure at his family home on Cape Cod. Doctors in Boston found that he had a type of brain tumor that is often fatal.

Kennedy *(center)* is surrounded by his family at the hospital in Boston in May 2008. *From left to right:* son Edward Kennedy Jr; son Patrick Kennedy, a member of the U.S. House of Representatives from Rhode Island; stepson Curran Raclin; Ted; daughter Kara Kennedy; wife Victoria; and stepdaughter Caroline Raclin.

Several days later, Kennedy had surgery to remove the tumor. And barely a month after that? Kennedy returned to the Senate, amidst great applause, to cast a decisive vote on an important Medicare bill. And showing his commitment to his country, he appeared at the Democratic National Convention in August to support

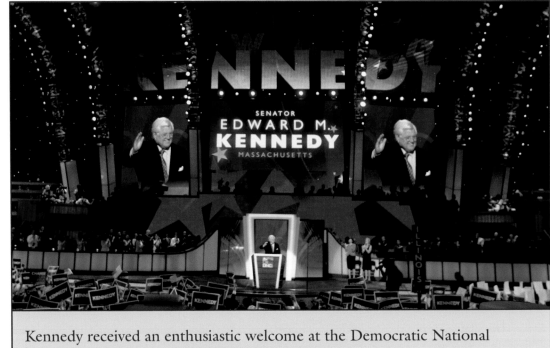

Kennedy received an enthusiastic welcome at the Democratic National Convention in August 2008. He rallied the Democratic Party for presidential candidate Barack Obama.

his friend, Barack Obama. "This November, the torch will be passed again to a new generation of Americans," he said. "For you and for me, for our country and for our cause—the work begins anew, the hope rises again, and the dream lives on."

The convention gave him even greater applause than he'd heard in the Senate: for the man, his courage, his spirit, and his determination to serve his country.

A History of the Kennedy Family

The Kennedy family has been known for generations for serving the United States in remarkable capacities. In addition to his grandparents and parents, many of Ted Kennedy's brothers and sisters contributed in special and important ways.

Honey "Fitz" Fitzgerald (1863–1950)—mayor of Boston

Joseph Kennedy (1888–1969)—ambassador to Great Britain

Rose Fitzgerald Kennedy (1890–1995)—designated papal countess

Joe Kennedy Jr. (1915–1944)—soldier killed while flying a special mission in World War II

John Kennedy (1917–1963)—thirty-fifth president of the United States

Rosemary Kennedy (1918–2005)—inspired siblings to help other people with mental disabilities

Kathleen Kennedy (1920–1948)—Red Cross volunteer during World War II

Eunice Kennedy Shriver (1921–)—founder of Special Olympics

Patricia Kennedy (1924–2006)—a founder of the National Committee for the Literary Arts

Robert Kennedy (1925–1968)—attorney general to President John F. Kennedy, U.S. senator from New York, candidate for presidential nomination

Jean Kennedy (1928–)—ambassador to Ireland (1993–1998)

Fun Facts about Ted Kennedy

★
★
★

- Ted Kennedy has good Senate company in keeping dogs in his offices. Senators Elizabeth Dole of North Carolina and Robert Byrd have had dogs in their offices too.

- Ted Kennedy had a costume party for his seventy-fifth birthday. He dressed as John Quincy Adams, the sixth president. Kennedy also throws costume parties for his staff. At past parties, he's impersonated Batman, a Milli Vanilli singer, and Elvis Presley.

- Ted Kennedy loved playing Santa Claus when his children were small. His son Teddy Jr. found him out when he said one day, "Santa, you have a bump on your cheek just like Daddy!"

- Ted Kennedy likes to grill outdoors. His favorites? Steaks and chicken and fish with tomatoes and marinade.

- Ted Kennedy also likes eggplant casserole, a Lebanese delicacy his wife makes.

- Ted Kennedy was almost a Green Bay Packer. Although the pro football team tried to recruit him back in 1955, he said that he was more interested in "another contact sport, politics."

- Ted Kennedy knows how to fly a plane. He learned when he was covering the western part of the United States for his brother Jack's presidential campaign.

- In 2006 Senator Kennedy's children's book called *My Senator and Me: A Dog's-Eye View of Washington, D.C.* was published. It was about a dog who accompanied his master to the Senate. Think it was based on a real dog?

- Ted Kennedy loves to listen to show tunes and opera.

- Ted Kennedy loves the Red Sox and celebrated when they "reversed the curse" to win the 2004 and 2007 World Series. His grandfather, Honey "Fitz" Fitzgerald, was one of the team's first Royal Rooters. This is a Red Sox fan club.

IMPORTANT DATES

1932	Edward M. Kennedy is born on February 22 in Boston to Joe and Rose Kennedy.
1958	He marries Joan Bennett on November 29 in Bronxville, New York.
1960	His first child, Kara Anne, is born on February 27.
1961	His second child, Edward Jr., is born on September 26.
1962	He won his first election to the U.S. Senate.
1963	President John F. Kennedy is assassinated in Dallas on November 22.
1964	He is injured in a plane crash on June 19.
1968	Robert Kennedy is assassinated in Los Angeles and dies on June 6.
1980	He runs for the Democratic nomination for U.S. president.
1992	On July 3, he marries Vicki Reggie.
2008	He is diagnosed with a brain tumor on May 20.

SOURCE NOTES

10 Edward M. Kennedy, *America Back on Track* (New York: Viking Penguin, 2006), 2.

12 Thomas Maier, *The Kennedys, America's Emerald Kings* (New York: Basic Books, 2003), 126.

13 Adam Clymer, *Edward M. Kennedy* (New York: William Morrow, 1999), 14.

22 *The Kennedys,* DVD (Boston: PBS, 2003).

23 Ibid.

26 Clymer, 59.

26 Clymer, 64.

27–29 *The Kennedys.*

29 Ibid.

30–31 Edward Kennedy, "Address to the People of Massachusetts on Chappaquiddick" (speech, broadcast on July 25, 1969).

31 Thomas Fields-Meyer, "The Torchbearer," *People,* August 16, 1999, 75.

31 Ibid.

32 Edward M. Kennedy, "Address to the Democratic National Convention" (speech, New York, August 12, 1980). Also quoted in David Espo, "Unlike Brothers, Ted Kennedy Grew Old in Public," *Boston Globe,* May 20, 2008.

33 Fox Butterfield, "AT HOME WITH: Ted and Vicki Kennedy; Crossed Paths, a Second Chance," *New York Times,* October 1, 1992.

33 Ibid.

34 Ibid.

34 Tom Gliatto, "Time to Marry? Right, Said Ted." *People,* March 30, 1992, 38.

40 Kennedy speech, Democratic National Convention, Denver, Colorado, August 25, 2008.

42 Ken Regan and George Howe Colt, "Is Ted Kennedy's Midlife Crisis Finally Over?" *Life,* August 1994, 48.

42 Edward M. Kennedy, "Almost a Green Bay Packer," n.d., http://kennedy.senate.gov/senator/index.cfm#packer (July 14, 2008).

FURTHER READING AND WEBSITES

John F. Kennedy Library
http://www.jfklibrary.org
His brother's archival library offers a great deal of information about Ted Kennedy, as well as audio of many of his key speeches.

Kennedy, Edward M. *America Back on Track.* New York: Viking Penguin, 2006. Kennedy wrote a book for adults proposing solutions for the United States' current problems in areas such as health care and energy.

Kennedy, Edward M. *My Senator and Me: A Dog's Eye View of Washington, D.C.* New York: Scholastic, 2006. Kennedy has written a book for young people on the political process through the eyes of his dogs.

The Kennedys
    http://www.pbs.org/wgbh/amex/kennedys/sfeature/sf_clymer
    .html
    Journalist and Ted Kennedy biographer Adam Clymer of the
    New York Times answers questions about the senator and his
    career.

Senator Edward M. Kennedy
    http://kennedy.senate.gov/senator/index.cfm
    The senator's own website offers biographical information, a
    political history, facts about national issues, and information
    for his Massachusetts constituents.

ACKNOWLEDGMENTS

Many thanks to Kitty Creswell at Lerner Publishing Group; Jean
Reynolds, my longtime friend and editor, especially for her support during my writing of this manuscript; Dean Roger Dennis
and faculty services librarian Peter Egler of the Earle Mack Drexel
University School of Law; Professor Alison Julien of Marquette Law
School; Professor Linda Edwards of Mercer and the University of
Nevada–Las Vegas Law Schools; and Professor Debby McGregor of
the Indiana University School of Law, for reading and commenting
on drafts of this manuscript and for offering support during the
writing process; the participants in the 2008 LWI Writers' Workshop
in Nashville, Indiana, for their important insights about and support
for an accurate portrayal of an important public figure; Stephen
McElroy, for encouraging me to continue writing about people I
admire; and my sweet, smart, super, savvy kids, Zoe and Abby

INDEX

Page numbers in *italics* refer to illustrations.